Contents

Some words are shown in bold, **like this**.
You can find out what they mean by looking
in the Glossary.

What is a coral reef?

A coral reef is like a huge rock-garden under the sea. A reef is made of billions of tiny sea-animals called **corals**.

Corals look like brightly coloured plants growing in the water.

What are...?

CORAL REEFS

Claire Llewellyn

Heinemann

3012201869510 2

For more information about Heinemann Library books, or to order, please telephone +44 (0)1865 888066, or send a fax to +44 (0)1865 314091. You can visit our web site at www.heinemann.co.uk

First published in Great Britain by Heinemann Library,
Halley Court, Jordan Hill, Oxford OX2 8EJ
a division of Reed Educational and Professional Publishing Ltd.
Heinemann is a registered trademark of Reed Educational & Professional Publishing Ltd.

OXFORD MELBOURNE AUCKLAND
JOHANNESBURG BLANTYRE GABORONE
IBADAN PORTSMOUTH (NH) USA CHICAGO

Designed by David Oakley
Illustrations by Hardlines and Jo Brooker
Printed by South China Printing Co.(1988) Ltd, Hong Kong / China

05 04 03 02 01
10 9 8 7 6 5 4 3 2 1

ISBN 0 431 02383 2

British Library Cataloguing in Publication Data
This book is also available in a hardback library edition (ISBN 0 431 02375 1)

Llewellyn, Claire
  What are coral reefs?
  1. Coral reefs and islands – Juvenile literature
  1. Title II. Coral reefs
  578.7'789

Acknowledgements
The Publishers would like to thank the following for permission to reproduce photographs: Bruce Coleman: Timothy O'Keefe p.20, Larry Lipsky p.29; FLPA: G Lebois p.5, Ian Cartwright p.7, Silvestris p.8, David B Fleetham p.10; NASA: Johnson Space Centre p.22, p.24, p.26; Oxford Scientific Films: David B Fleetham p.6, p.16, Mark Webster p.14, Laurence Gould p.18; Robert Harding Picture Library: p.21; Still Pictures: Fred Bavendam p.4, Gerard & Margi Moss p.9, p.11, p.13, Truchet-Unep p.12, Yves Lefevre p.15, Norbert Wu p.17, Alberto Garcias/Christian Aid p.19, Roland Seitre p.28.

Cover photograph reproduced with permission of Still Pictures.

Every effort has been made to contact copyright holders of any material reproduced in this book. Any omissions will be rectified in subsequent printings if notice is given to the Publisher.

A coral reef looks like rocks under the water.

Most coral reefs are found in sunny, shallow waters in the warmest parts of the world.

How do reefs grow?

Corals have soft bodies, and grow hard **skeletons** to protect themselves. The tiny skeleton is shaped like a cup.

Corals grow in many different shapes and colours. This is antler coral.

Coral reefs can take thousands of years to grow.

When the old corals die, their skeletons stay on the reef. New corals grow on top of them. Slowly, the reef begins to grow.

Where do reefs grow?

These coral reefs are around islands in the Indian Ocean.

Most coral reefs grow in the warm, shallow water around islands or along the coast.

The coral reefs help to protect the coast from high waves and stormy seas.

Waves break on the reef. The water between the reef and the land is calm.

Barrier reefs

Some coral reefs lie in deeper water and grow in a line along the coast. They are called barrier reefs because they make a barrier between the land and the sea.

The Great Barrier Reef off Australia is as high as a 40-storey building.

The waters in a **lagoon** are calmer than the choppy sea.

The sea-water between the reef and the shore is called a lagoon. It is protected from the wind and waves of the sea.

A coral island

Many islands are the **peaks** of **volcanoes** under the sea. Sometimes a volcano sinks down below the waves because of movements deep inside the Earth.

This island is the top of a volcano.
A coral reef has grown all around it.

There was once an island in the middle of this ring of coral. But now it has sunk below the waves and disappeared.

The coral reef that once grew around the island remains as a ring of rocks.

Rainforests of the sea

Coral reefs are often called the rainforests of the sea. This is because they are home to thousands of different living things.

A coral reef is crowded and full of life.

Grey sharks hunt the animals that
live on a coral reef.

Small animals live on the reef, feeding on
smaller animals or plants. Larger animals
visit the reef to find food.

Reefs in danger

Rough seas batter and break a coral reef.

Coral is hard and stony, but it is still easy to break. It cracks during storms when it is pounded by the sea.

The crown-of-thorns starfish feeds on coral. In one day a crown-of-thorns starfish eats enough coral to cover a small table. This much coral can take 100 years to grow.

The crow-of-thorns starfish can be a danger to a reef.

Human damage

Some divers make money by collecting and selling pieces of coral.

People also damage coral reefs. **Corals** die when divers stand on a reef, knock it with an **anchor**, or break off bits to sell.

Hunters catch the animals and fish that live in coral reefs and sell them. Some of the fish are now very rare because they have been hunted too much.

This fisherman has caught a tropical fish to sell as a pet.

Saving the reefs

Coral reefs need to be protected. One way of doing this is to turn them into underwater **Marine Parks**. They are protected by law.

DO NOT STAND ON ANY CORAL
It is a fragile animal form, easily killed

This coral reef is in the US Virgin Islands. It is now a Marine Park.

These people are learning to dive
so that they can visit a coral reef.

People visit the reefs and see the animals
and plants that live there. They learn how
to protect the reefs.

Reef map 1

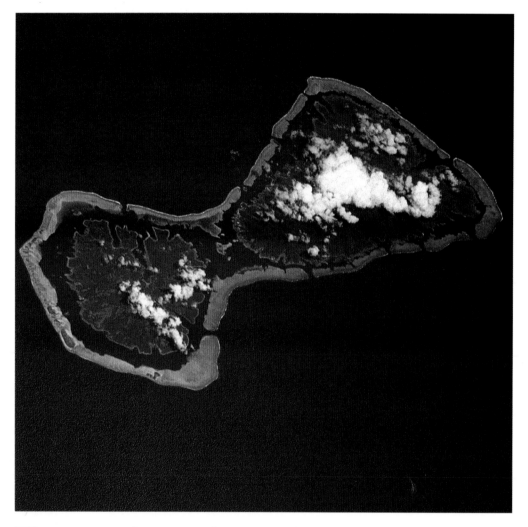

This is a photo of a small island. It was taken from a **satellite**. Coral reefs have grown all round the island. There are **lagoons** between the reefs and the shore.

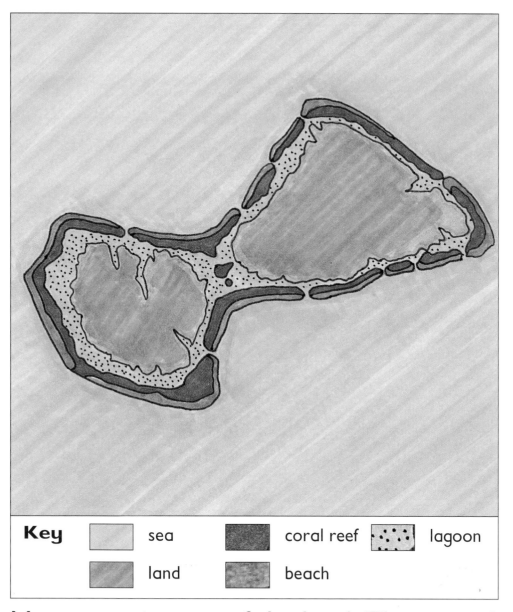

Key   sea   coral reef   lagoon

land   beach

Maps are pictures of the land. This map shows us the same place as the photo. The coral reefs are shown with purple. You can see beaches around the reefs. They are orange.

Reef map 2

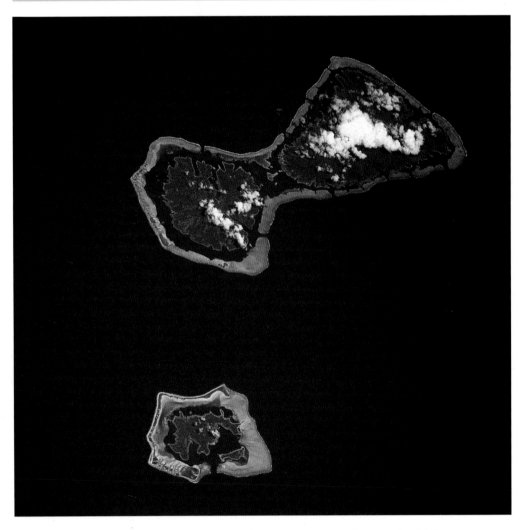

This photo shows the same island. The island looks smaller but you can see more of the sea around it. You can see a second island. It has coral around it too.

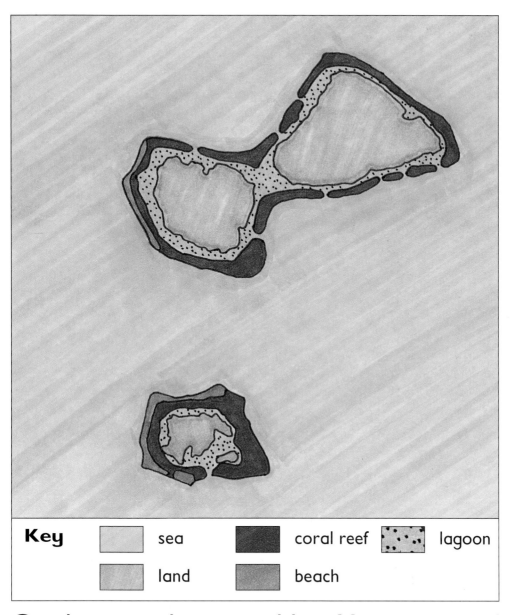

Key

sea	coral reef	lagoon
land	beach	

On the map the sea is blue. You can see the spotted blue between the coral reef and the land. This is called a **lagoon**. The water here is shallow and sheltered.

Reef map 3

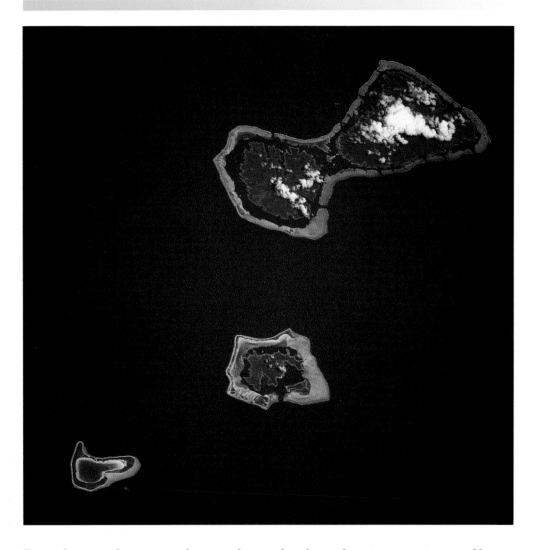

In this photo the islands look even smaller.
Now you can see a third coral island near by.
This third island is only made of a coral reef
ring. The islands look like big dots in the sea.

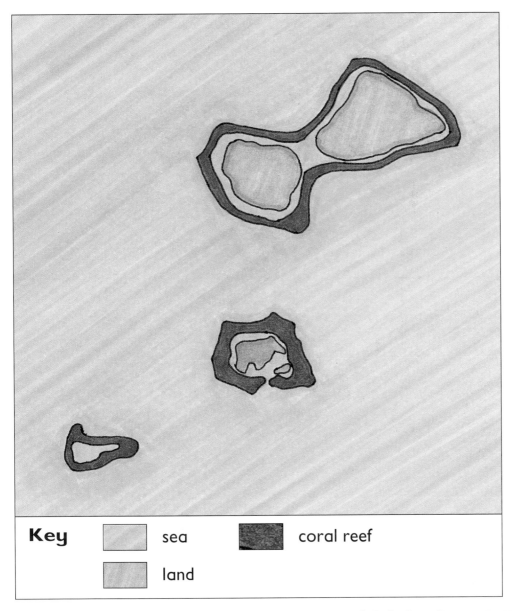

Key

sea   coral reef

land

Maps give useful information. With this map it is easy to see how far the islands are from one another. You can also see which island is the biggest.

Amazing reef facts

The Great Barrier Reef is a long line of reefs off the coast of Australia. Altogether, it covers more land than the whole of the United Kingdom.

The wrinkly coral on the left of the picture is called brain coral.

This coral reef is growing in Florida, USA. Florida is cooler than most places **corals** grow, but the sea here is warm. It flows up from the hotter parts of the world.

Glossary

anchor   a tool that holds a ship in one place. It catches in the sea-bed.

corals   tiny animals that live in the sea. Their skeletons build coral reefs.

lagoon   the sheltered water that lies between a barrier reef and the shore

Marine Park   an underwater place protected by law to keep it safe and beautiful

peak   the very top of a mountain

satellite   a special machine which goes around the Earth in space. It can take photographs of the Earth.

skeleton   the hard part of an animal's body that protects it and gives it its shape

volcano   a mountain that is still being made. It sometimes erupts, shooting out hot rock and ash from inside the Earth. Some volcanoes are on the sea-bed.

More books to read

Carole Telford and Rod Theodorou. *Amazing Journeys: Inside a Coral Reef.* Heinemann, 1997

Nicola Baxter. *Our Wonderful Earth.* Two-Can, 1997

Andy Owen and Miranda Ashwell. *What Are... Seas and Oceans?* Heinemann, 1998

F. Brooks and K. Khanduri. *First Encyclopedia of our World.* Usborne, 1999

Index